Jupiter

CHERRY LAKE PRESS

Published in the United States of America by Cherry Lake Publishing
Ann Arbor, Michigan
www.cherrylakepublishing.com

Reading Adviser: Marla Conn, MS, Ed, Literacy specialist, Read-Ability, Inc.
Book Designer: Jennifer Wahi
Illustrator: Jeff Bane

Photo Credits: ©PIA22946/NASA, 5; ©Vadim Sadovski/Shutterstock, 7, 11, 17, 19; ©Tristan3D/Shutterstock, 9; ©PIA22949/NASA, 13; ©Caltech/SwRI/MSSS/ Gerald Eichstädt /Seán Doran/NASA, 15; ©Sergey Nivens/ Shutterstock, 21; ©NASA images/Shutterstock, 23; Cover, 2-3,12, 18, 22, Jeff Bane; Various vector images throughout courtesy of Shutterstock.com/

Library of Congress Cataloging-in-Publication Data

Names: Devera, Czeena, author. | Bane, Jeff, 1957- illustrator. | Devera,
   Czeena. My guide to the planets.
Title: Jupiter / by Czeena Devera ; illustrated by Jeff Bane.
Description: Ann Arbor, Michigan : Cherry Lake Publishing, [2020] | Series:
   My guide to the planets | Includes index. | Audience: K-1.
Identifiers: LCCN 2019032911 (print) | LCCN 2019032912 (ebook) | ISBN
   9781534158887 (hardcover) | ISBN 9781534161184 (paperback) | ISBN
   9781534160033 (pdf) | ISBN 9781534162334 (ebook)
Subjects: LCSH: Jupiter (Planet)--Juvenile literature.
Classification: LCC QB661 .D48 2020 (print) | LCC QB661 (ebook) | DDC
   523.45--dc23
LC record available at https://lccn.loc.gov/2019032911
LC ebook record available at https://lccn.loc.gov/2019032912

Printed in the United States of America
Corporate Graphics

About the author: Czeena Devera grew up in the red-hot heat of Arizona surrounded by books. Her childhood bedroom had built-in bookshelves that were always full. She now lives in Michigan with an even bigger library of books.

About the illustrator: Jeff Bane and his two business partners own a studio along the American River in Folsom, California, home of the 1849 Gold Rush. When Jeff's not sketching or illustrating for clients, he's either swimming or kayaking in the river to relax.

I'm Jupiter. I'm the fifth-closest planet to the Sun.

I'm the largest planet in the **solar system**.

I am so large that 11 Earths could fit across my **equator**.

I **orbit** around the Sun. It takes me almost 12 years to complete 1 orbit!

I am one of the four **gas giants**.

Gas giants are mostly made up of gases. I don't have solid ground like Earth.

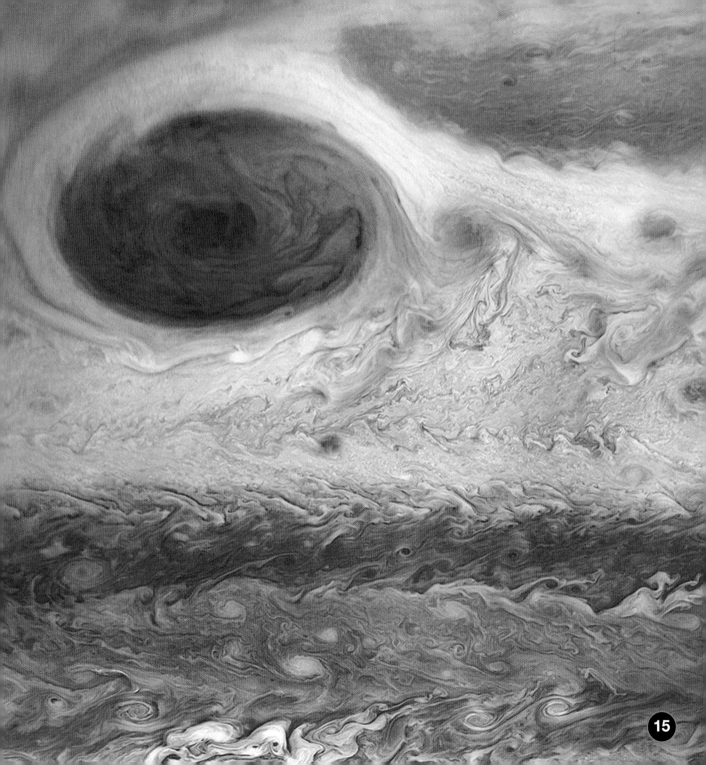

I have four rings that surround me. They are made from **asteroid** dust.

I have 79 moons. That's a lot compared to Earth!

One day, my moons might support life!

I am a **unique** planet. There are still new things to discover about me.

glossary

asteroid (AS-tuh-roid) small, rocky object that travels around the sun

equator (ih-KWAY-tur) an imaginary line around the middle of a planet

gas giants (GAS JYE-uhnts) planets that are made up mostly of gases and are not solid

orbit (OR-bit) to travel in a curved path around something

solar system (SOH-lur SIS-tuhm) the Sun and all the things that orbit around it, like planets

unique (yoo-NEEK) the only one of its kind

index